BECOMING OK

Prologue

Life doesn't stay still. The moment you think you've found solid ground, something shifts. The plans you made, the clarity you achieved, the alignment you worked so hard to create—none of it stays fixed. And that's not a failure. It's the nature of being alive. Life is motion, and motion is becoming.

Becoming is not about arriving at a destination. It's not about finally being "OK" in some permanent, unchanging way. Becoming is a process, a rhythm, a constant interplay between stability and chaos, clarity and dissonance. It's about learning to live within the motion, to embrace it, to let it guide you instead of resisting its pull. To become OK is not to stop the movement—it's to find your balance within it.

This book is about that balance. It's about learning to navigate the flux of life, to see change not as something to be feared but as something to work with. It's about recognizing that alignment isn't a one-time achievement—it's something you recalibrate again and again as you grow, as you learn, as the world shifts around you. Becoming OK isn't about perfection—it's about engagement. It's about showing up for the process, moment by moment.

The process of becoming asks you to let go of the illusion of control. It asks you to step into the rhythm of life's motion and trust that the steps you take—imperfect, uncertain, incomplete —are enough. It asks you to embrace curiosity over certainty, flexibility over rigidity, presence over destination. Becoming isn't about having all the answers—it's about learning to live with the questions, to let them shape you, to let them guide you toward something more.

This isn't a book about solving every problem or finding a perfect path. It's a book about learning to live in the in-between spaces, the places where clarity and chaos meet, where dissonance and alignment coexist. It's about seeing the cracks not as flaws but as openings, the tension not as something to fix but as something to embrace, the motion not as something to control but as something to flow with.

To become OK is to recognize that life is not a static state but a dynamic dance. It's to see yourself not as a finished product but as an unfolding process. It's to understand that the work of being OK isn't about eliminating the dissonance or achieving some final version of harmony—it's about learning to move within it, to let it deepen you, to let it become part of your rhythm.

This is where the journey continues. From stability to dissonance, from dissonance to motion, from motion to growth. The path isn't straight, and it isn't always clear. But it's alive, and so are you. Becoming OK is not about where you end—it's about how you move, how you adapt, how you grow. It's about learning to live, fully and authentically, within the dynamic, ever-changing rhythm of being alive.

Chapter 1: The Wave of Becoming
Section A: The Ebb and Flow

Life in Motion

L ife doesn't sit still. It moves, always. Even in the moments that feel quiet, even in the pauses between events, there is motion. Breath flows in and out. Days begin and end. The currents of your thoughts shift, sometimes gently, sometimes with the force of a storm. Life moves like a wave, surging forward, receding, and then building again, carrying you in its rhythm whether you notice it or not.

This motion is both comforting and unsettling. It promises that nothing stays the same, that even the hardest moments will pass. But it also reminds you that the stable ground you seek can never be fully permanent. The wave doesn't stop—it doesn't let you stay in one place forever. Stability is always temporary, always dynamic, always part of the larger rhythm of motion.

At first, this realization can feel disorienting. It's natural to want things to stay steady, to find a place where you can rest without worrying that the ground beneath you will shift again. But the wave doesn't stop, and learning to live within its rhythm is not about finding an unchanging anchor—it's about learning to move with the flow. It's about seeing the motion not as something to fight, but as something to work with, something to trust.

The ebb and flow of life are not random. They follow patterns, rhythms that may not always be visible but are always present. The moments of surging forward, when clarity and energy are abundant, are followed by moments of retreat, when reflection and rest become necessary. The wave doesn't apologize for its motion—it simply moves, creating balance through its cycles.

To live within the wave is to recognize these cycles and to trust them. The retreat is not a failure—it's part of the rhythm. The surge is not a guarantee—it's part of the flow. The wave teaches you that becoming isn't about staying in one state forever—it's about engaging with the constant motion, allowing it to carry you, shape you, and guide you toward something deeper.

Riding the Currents

To live is to move. It's to be carried by the currents of life, even when you don't feel ready, even when you'd rather stay still. The wave doesn't wait for your permission—it flows, and you flow with it. The question isn't whether you'll move; it's how you'll choose to move. Will you fight against the currents, exhausting yourself in the process, or will you learn to ride them, finding balance even as the motion carries you somewhere new?

Riding the currents doesn't mean giving up control. It means understanding that control is not the same as resistance. The wave doesn't ask you to surrender—it asks you to engage. It asks you to notice its rhythms, to feel the push and pull of its motion, to align yourself with its flow rather than struggling against it. The wave isn't something to conquer—it's something to collaborate with.

This collaboration begins with awareness. To ride the currents, you have to first notice them. What are the patterns in your life? Where do you feel the surges of energy, the moments of clarity and movement? Where do you feel the retreats, the pauses, the spaces that call for rest and reflection? The wave is always moving, but it's not random. It has a rhythm, and when you learn to tune into that rhythm, you begin to find your balance within it.

Balance within the wave isn't static—it's dynamic. It's about adjusting to the motion, shifting your weight, finding your center even as the ground beneath you moves. It's about accepting that stability within the wave isn't about stopping the motion—it's about moving with it. It's about recognizing that the flow of life is not something you have to control, but something you can trust.

Riding the currents means letting go of the need for certainty. It means embracing the idea that you won't always know where the wave is taking you, but that you can navigate it one moment at a time. It's about focusing not on the destination, but on the process —on the act of moving, of adjusting, of becoming. The wave doesn't ask you to be perfect—it asks you to be present. And in that presence, you find your rhythm.

The wave of becoming is not a challenge to overcome—it's a truth to live within. To ride its currents is to engage fully with the motion of life, to see its rhythms not as something to fear but as something to trust. The wave carries you forward, always, and as you move with it, you begin to see that the motion itself is where life's beauty and meaning reside.

Section B: Riding the Currents
Embracing Motion

To embrace motion is to accept that life is inherently dynamic. There is no stillness that lasts, no stability that endures forever. The currents of life are always shifting, always carrying you forward into new experiences, new challenges, new opportunities for growth. This motion isn't something to fear—it's something to understand, to work with, to embrace.

The instinct, when faced with life's motion, is often to hold on tightly to what feels stable, to resist the pull of change, to anchor yourself in the familiar. But resistance doesn't stop the motion. It only makes the ride more turbulent. The wave doesn't pause because you're not ready—it moves, and the more you resist, the more you feel its force. Embracing motion means loosening your grip, allowing yourself to flow with the currents rather than fighting against them.

This isn't about passivity. Embracing motion doesn't mean giving up or letting the wave carry you wherever it pleases. It means engaging with the motion, finding your balance within it, and steering when you can. It means learning to feel the rhythm of the wave, to notice its cycles, to understand when to push forward and when to pull back. It means accepting that motion is not something to control—it's something to collaborate with.

To embrace motion is also to embrace uncertainty. The wave doesn't show you where it's going—it only shows you the next moment, the next rise or fall, the next surge or retreat. This uncertainty can feel unsettling, but it's also liberating. It frees you from the need to have all the answers, to know exactly where you're going or how you'll get there. It invites you to focus on the present moment, on the act of moving, on the process of becoming.

When you embrace motion, you begin to see the beauty in its unpredictability. You start to trust that the wave will carry you, not always where you expect, but always where you need to go. You stop clinging to the idea of permanence and start finding your balance in the flow. You learn that motion isn't something that happens to you—it's something you are a part of. It's the rhythm of life itself.

Trusting the Flow

Motion is unsettling because it refuses to promise certainty. It doesn't guarantee you'll land exactly where you want to, nor does it provide a roadmap for how to get there. The wave moves, and you move with it, sometimes in sync, sometimes struggling to find your footing. But motion doesn't require certainty to be meaningful—it requires trust. To ride the currents is to trust the flow, to believe that the motion itself holds value, even when the destination isn't clear.

Trusting the flow doesn't mean abandoning intention. It doesn't mean letting the currents carry you without awareness or care. It means bringing your presence, your curiosity, your values into the motion. It means recognizing that while you can't control the wave, you can guide how you engage with it. You can steer, adjust, recalibrate—not to resist the flow, but to work with it, shaping its rhythm into something that aligns with who you are and what you need.

This trust is not blind. It's built on the understanding that the wave, as unpredictable as it feels, is not random. Life's motion follows patterns, rhythms that reflect the interplay of clarity and chaos, stability and dissonance. The rise and fall of the wave, the ebb and flow of its currents, mirror the cycles of your own experience. Moments of progress are followed by moments of pause, moments of clarity by moments of doubt. The motion may feel chaotic, but within it, there is a deeper order—a rhythm that carries you forward even when it feels like you're standing still.

Trusting the flow also means accepting the moments when the wave takes you somewhere unexpected. It means allowing for the possibility that what lies ahead may be different than what you imagined, and that this difference may hold its own beauty, its own meaning. It means letting go of the need to control every outcome, to predict every turn, to protect yourself from every unknown. Trust isn't about certainty—it's about openness. It's about believing that the wave, in its motion, will teach you what you need to learn.

This openness is what transforms motion from something to endure into something to embrace. When you trust the flow, you begin to see the wave not as a force working against you, but as a partner in the process of becoming. The motion no longer feels like chaos—it feels like possibility. Each rise and fall becomes an opportunity to learn, to adapt, to grow. Each shift in the current becomes a chance to realign, to reconnect, to reimagine.

To trust the flow is to trust yourself. It's to believe that you have the capacity to navigate the wave, even when it feels overwhelming. It's to remember that motion isn't something to fear—it's something to live within, something to move with, something to create with. The wave doesn't ask for perfection— it asks for presence. And in that presence, you find your rhythm, your balance, your way forward.

Trusting the flow doesn't mean the motion will always feel smooth. There will be moments when the currents pull harder than you expected, when the direction shifts suddenly, when the rhythm feels impossible to find. But the wave keeps moving, and so do you. And with each moment of trust, with each step into the flow, you begin to see that the motion isn't taking you away from yourself—it's bringing you closer to who you are becoming.

Chapter 2: The Dance of Opposites
Section A: Holding the Tension

The Creative Power of Contradiction

Life is built on opposites. Light and dark, order and chaos, stillness and motion—these contrasts are not just features of existence; they are its foundation. Without one, the other loses its meaning. Light is only understood in the context of shadow, motion in the context of stillness. Opposites don't cancel each other out—they define each other, creating a dynamic interplay that gives life its depth and richness.

But living within this interplay isn't always comfortable. Opposites create tension, and tension demands attention. It asks you to hold the space between two forces that seem to pull in different directions, each one carrying its own truth, its own needs, its own demands. This tension feels like a contradiction, a choice you must make between two incompatible paths. But the truth is, opposites are not enemies—they are partners in creation.

The tension between opposites is not something to resolve—it's something to embrace. It's not about choosing light over dark, order over chaos, stillness over motion. It's about recognizing that both are necessary, that both are part of the same whole. The tension isn't a problem—it's a source of energy, a creative force that drives transformation and growth. Without tension, there is no movement, no change, no becoming.

To hold the tension is to resist the urge to collapse it into a single answer. It's to stand in the space between opposites, allowing both to exist without trying to eliminate one or the other. This isn't easy. The human mind craves resolution, clarity, certainty. It wants to know which side is right, which path is correct, which force will win. But the dance of opposites isn't about resolution —it's about relationship. It's about seeing how the opposites interact, how they shape and influence each other, how they create something greater together than they could apart.

The creative power of contradiction lies in its ability to expand your perspective. When you hold the tension between opposites, you begin to see beyond binary choices. You start to notice the nuances, the possibilities that exist in the overlap, the spaces where light and dark, order and chaos, stillness and motion converge. These spaces are not contradictions—they are invitations. They ask you to think differently, to feel deeply, to create something new.

Holding the tension doesn't mean avoiding action. It doesn't mean staying stuck in indecision, paralyzed by the fear of making the wrong choice. It means moving with awareness, with the understanding that both sides of the tension have something to teach you. It means asking: *What can this tension reveal? What new perspective, new possibility, new harmony might emerge if I let both forces have their say?* The tension isn't an obstacle—it's a doorway. And when you step through it, you find a new way of seeing, a new way of being.

Finding Strength in Balance

Tension feels uncomfortable because it resists resolution. It pulls you in different directions, asking you to hold truths that seem to contradict each other. The instinct is to resolve it, to tip the balance in favor of one side, to settle the argument and move forward. But true balance doesn't come from erasing tension—it comes from finding strength within it, from learning to hold the opposites without collapsing them into simplicity.

Strength in balance isn't about compromise. It's not about choosing the middle ground or diluting the intensity of either side. It's about letting both forces exist fully, honoring what each brings to the whole. The light and the dark, the clarity and the chaos, the stillness and the motion—these aren't enemies to be reconciled. They are partners, each contributing something essential to the dynamic interplay of life.

This balance isn't static. It shifts, adjusts, moves with the rhythm of your experiences. Some days, the light shines brighter, illuminating your path with clarity and confidence. Other days, the shadows deepen, asking you to sit with uncertainty, to navigate the unknown. Both are necessary. Both are valuable. To find strength in balance is to trust the rhythm, to know that the light will return when you're in the dark and that the stillness will ground you when the motion feels overwhelming.

The tension between opposites isn't just something you endure —it's something you can use. The pull of the opposites creates energy, a force that drives creativity, innovation, and growth. It challenges you to think beyond binaries, to find solutions and perspectives that wouldn't exist if you stayed on one side of the tension. The strength of balance lies in its ability to expand your perspective, to show you that the opposites are not in competition —they are in collaboration.

To find balance within tension is to ask yourself: *What is each side of this tension offering me? What can I learn from the pull of each force? How might holding both create something new, something deeper, something more aligned?* These questions don't resolve the tension—they engage with it. They transform the discomfort of the pull into the power of the push, turning opposition into momentum.

The balance isn't always perfect, and it doesn't need to be. The strength of balance lies not in achieving a flawless equilibrium but in being willing to adjust, to shift, to recalibrate as the rhythm of life changes. It's about staying present with the tension, trusting that it's not here to break you but to build you, to deepen you, to guide you toward a harmony that includes all of who you are.

When you find strength in balance, the tension becomes less about conflict and more about connection. The opposites don't pull you apart—they hold you together. They create a space where complexity can thrive, where the light and the dark, the clarity and the chaos, the stillness and the motion come together to create the depth, the richness, the beauty of life.

Section B: The Space Between
The Creative Tension

The space between opposites is where creation happens. It's not in the clarity of one truth or the dominance of one force, but in the interplay, the overlap, the dance between the two. This space can feel unstable, uncertain, even chaotic. It's the moment before resolution, the pause between breaths, the edge of what you understand and what you don't. But within this space lies potential—potential for something new, something unexpected, something transformative.

Creative tension arises when opposites meet and begin to interact. It's the push and pull between stability and motion, between order and chaos, between the known and the unknown. This tension isn't comfortable, but it's productive. It generates energy, asking you to step beyond what feels safe or familiar and to engage with the possibilities that exist in the middle. The space between isn't a void—it's a spark.

This spark doesn't extinguish the opposites—it brings them into conversation. It allows light and shadow, clarity and ambiguity, stillness and motion to inform one another, to shape one another, to create something greater together than they could apart. The tension isn't something to resolve—it's something to explore. It's a field of possibilities, a place where contradictions don't cancel each other out but combine to create something entirely new.

Living in the space between opposites requires curiosity. It asks you to let go of certainty, to embrace the questions instead of rushing toward answers. *What happens when stability meets motion? What insights emerge when light and dark share the same space? What new paths open when clarity and ambiguity converge?* These questions don't demand immediate solutions—they invite exploration. They remind you that growth isn't about choosing one side—it's about learning from both.

The creative tension in the space between opposites isn't about perfection. It's messy, dynamic, unpredictable. But it's also alive, filled with energy and movement. It's the space where life becomes art, where the pieces you thought were incompatible come together to form something coherent, something beautiful, something entirely your own.

Where Possibility Emerges

The space between opposites isn't empty—it's alive. It pulses with energy, tension, and possibility, creating a fertile ground where transformation begins. This space is where growth happens, not because it's comfortable or certain, but because it's dynamic. It's a place where stability and chaos, light and shadow, clarity and ambiguity collide, generating the sparks of something new. It is a liminal space, a threshold where what was meets what could be.

At first, this space can feel unsettling. It's neither one thing nor the other, neither the comfort of the known nor the clarity of the resolved. It's the in-between, the unresolved, the ambiguous. But this ambiguity isn't a void—it's a field of infinite potential. It's where ideas form, where connections emerge, where possibilities take shape. The space between isn't a place to avoid—it's a place to dwell.

Dwelling in this space requires patience. It's tempting to rush through it, to seek resolution, to collapse the tension into something easier to hold. But the space between isn't something to rush—it's something to explore. It asks you to slow down, to notice the patterns, to feel the energy of the opposites at play. It asks you to resist the urge to choose a side and instead to see how the sides interact, how they shape each other, how they create something greater together than they could apart.

This space is where contradictions find their balance. It's where light and shadow converge to create depth, where stability and motion meet to create rhythm, where clarity and ambiguity blend to create texture. It's not about eliminating the tension between opposites—it's about harnessing it, using it as a source of creativity, insight, and transformation. The tension isn't something to fix—it's something to work with.

To live in the space between opposites is to become comfortable with uncertainty. It's to trust that the discomfort of not knowing is part of the process, part of the unfolding. It's to believe that the opposites you're holding—however contradictory they feel—are part of the same whole, and that the space between them isn't a gap, but a bridge. This trust doesn't erase the discomfort, but it transforms it into something meaningful, something powerful, something alive.

The space between is where possibility emerges. It's where you discover not just who you are, but who you are becoming. It's where the questions that feel unanswerable lead to insights you couldn't have imagined. It's where the parts of yourself that seem disconnected find their way back together. The space between isn't just a place of tension—it's a place of connection, creation, and becoming.

To dwell in the space between is to embrace life's complexity. It's to see that opposites aren't enemies, but partners. It's to understand that the light needs the shadow, the stability needs the motion, the clarity needs the ambiguity. It's to realize that the beauty of life isn't in resolving the opposites, but in dancing with them, in letting their interplay create the rhythm of your becoming.

Chapter 3: The Compass of Change
Section A: Orienting in Uncertainty

Finding Your Bearings

Change is disorienting. It sweeps in like an unexpected tide, pulling you away from the familiar and leaving you adrift in waters that feel uncharted. The structures you relied on, the routines that grounded you, the plans that gave you direction—they all shift under the weight of change. And in their place, you're left with uncertainty, a vast expanse where you're no longer sure which way is forward or what "forward" even means.

When you're caught in the currents of change, the first instinct is to look outward, to search for something solid, something fixed that can guide you back to stability. But in moments of upheaval, the external world often offers no such anchor. The familiar landmarks have shifted, and the paths you used to follow no longer lead where they once did. The compass you need isn't out there—it's within you.

Finding your bearings in uncertainty begins with presence. It's not about rushing to make sense of the change or forcing yourself into action—it's about pausing long enough to notice where you are. What does this moment feel like? What is this change asking of you? What emotions are rising to the surface, and what might they be telling you about what matters most? Orientation isn't about having all the answers—it's about starting with what you know and letting it guide you toward what you don't.

The inner compass isn't a map—it's a sense of direction. It's the part of you that knows your values, your priorities, your deeper truths. When the external world feels chaotic, this inner compass becomes your guide, not by telling you exactly where to go, but by pointing you toward alignment. It asks you to trust yourself, to trust that even in the midst of uncertainty, you have the capacity to navigate the change, one step at a time.

To orient yourself in uncertainty is to anchor yourself in what doesn't change: your values, your resilience, your capacity to adapt. It's to recognize that while the circumstances around you may shift, the core of who you are remains steady. And from that steadiness, you can begin to chart a path forward—not a perfect path, not a complete path, but a path that feels true to the moment you're in.

Anchoring in Motion

When everything around you shifts, it's natural to feel unmoored. Change has a way of disrupting not just the external patterns of your life, but the internal ones—the sense of who you are, what you stand for, and where you're going. It pulls at the edges of your identity, asking questions you may not feel ready to answer. *Who am I now, in this new reality? What matters when everything feels uncertain? How do I find my way forward when the path behind me is gone?*

In these moments, the idea of anchoring can feel like an impossibility. What can you hold onto when nothing feels stable? What can guide you when the landmarks you once trusted have shifted or disappeared? The answer lies not in finding something outside of yourself to cling to, but in creating an internal anchor —a compass that grounds you in your values, your priorities, and your capacity to adapt.

Anchoring in motion is about finding steadiness within yourself, even as the world around you continues to shift. It's about recognizing that you don't need to have all the answers to move forward—you just need to know what matters most. Your values become your anchor, reminding you of who you are and what you stand for. Your ability to adapt becomes your strength, allowing you to navigate change with flexibility and grace.

But anchoring isn't about staying still. It's not about resisting the motion or trying to stop the currents of change. It's about creating a sense of stability within the motion, a way of orienting yourself even as the waves carry you in unexpected directions. The anchor doesn't stop the tide—it grounds you within it, reminding you that you have the tools to navigate whatever comes next.

This process begins with clarity. What do you value? What feels non-negotiable in this moment of change? What truths about yourself remain steady, even as the circumstances around you evolve? These questions aren't about fixing everything at once—

they're about giving yourself a starting point, a way to orient yourself in the midst of uncertainty.

From this clarity, you can begin to make choices—not perfect choices, not final choices, but intentional ones. Anchoring in motion means allowing yourself to move forward one step at a time, trusting that each step will bring you closer to the alignment you seek. It's about focusing not on the destination, but on the process, on the act of choosing, of engaging, of continuing to move even when the path isn't fully visible.

To anchor in motion is to trust yourself. It's to believe that even in the midst of uncertainty, you have the capacity to adapt, to recalibrate, to create meaning from the changes you're experiencing. It's to remember that the compass you need isn't out there—it's within you, always pointing you toward what feels true, even when the path is unclear.

This trust doesn't erase the discomfort of change, but it transforms it. It reminds you that uncertainty isn't the absence of direction—it's the space where direction is created. And as you anchor yourself within the motion, you begin to see that the waves of change aren't carrying you away from yourself—they're carrying you closer to who you're becoming.

Section B: Adapting in Motion
The Art of Adjusting

Adaptation is the art of staying connected to yourself while the world around you changes. It's not about bending to every shift or losing yourself in the chaos—it's about learning how to adjust, how to pivot, how to move in ways that align with your values, even when the ground beneath you feels unstable. Adapting isn't about control—it's about creativity. It's about finding new ways to navigate the currents of life without losing sight of who you are.

The first step in adapting is to let go of the need for permanence. Change is unsettling because it disrupts the illusion of stability, the belief that things should stay the same, that the plans you made should unfold exactly as you envisioned. But life doesn't work that way. Motion is its natural state, and adaptation means learning to move with it instead of resisting it. Letting go of permanence doesn't mean giving up—it means freeing yourself to respond to what's happening, rather than clinging to what was.

Adaptation also requires flexibility—not just in your actions, but in your mindset. When things don't go as planned, when the currents shift unexpectedly, the ability to adjust your perspective becomes just as important as adjusting your path. What if this change isn't a setback but an opportunity? What if this challenge is asking you to grow in ways you hadn't considered? Flexibility doesn't erase the discomfort of change, but it opens the door to possibility.

But adaptation isn't just about responding to external changes—it's about aligning with your internal rhythm. It's about checking in with yourself, asking: *What do I need in this moment? What feels true to me right now?* Adapting in motion means staying connected to your values, your priorities, your deeper truths, even as you adjust to the shifting circumstances around you. It's about finding ways to move forward that feel authentic, even if they don't look like the path you originally imagined.

Adapting doesn't mean you have to have everything figured out. It's not about perfection or certainty—it's about engagement. It's about being willing to try, to experiment, to take one step, and then another, and then another, trusting that the act of moving will bring clarity over time. The art of adjusting isn't a one-time skill—it's an ongoing practice, one that evolves with you as you navigate the waves of change.

The Dance of Flexibility

Adaptation isn't just a skill—it's a dance. It's the ability to move with life's shifting rhythms, to flow with its unexpected turns, to adjust your steps without losing your balance. The dance of flexibility isn't about abandoning your direction—it's about finding new ways to align with it. It's about recognizing that the path you thought you'd take might not be the one that carries you forward, and that's not failure—it's motion.

Flexibility begins with listening. Change speaks to you, not always in words, but in feelings, patterns, and moments of tension. It whispers through the discomfort of a situation that no longer feels aligned, the frustration of a plan that isn't working, the pull of a possibility you hadn't considered. To adapt is to listen to these signals, to let them guide you toward what needs to shift, what needs to soften, what needs to expand.

This dance isn't always graceful. Flexibility asks you to stretch, sometimes into unfamiliar or uncomfortable spaces. It asks you to try new steps, to let go of old routines, to trust that the rhythm you're learning will support you even if it feels awkward at first. Adaptation isn't about getting it right the first time—it's about staying in the movement, adjusting as you go, finding your footing again and again.

The dance of flexibility also requires trust—trust in yourself, trust in the process, trust in the rhythm of life itself. Change often feels chaotic because it doesn't unfold according to your timeline or expectations. But flexibility reminds you that the rhythm isn't random—it's responsive. The steps you take shape the music you hear, and the way you move within the change influences where it takes you. Trusting the dance means believing that even when the rhythm feels unfamiliar, it's leading you somewhere meaningful.

Flexibility isn't just about external adjustments—it's about internal alignment. It's about asking yourself: *What am I holding onto that no longer serves me? What am I resisting that might help me grow? What do I need to let go of to move forward?* These questions aren't easy, but they create space for clarity. They remind you that adapting isn't about abandoning yourself—it's about reconnecting with who you are in the midst of change.

The dance of flexibility teaches you that movement isn't linear—it's fluid. It ebbs and flows, rises and falls, shifts and sways. It's not about finding the "right" step—it's about finding the step that feels aligned in this moment, knowing that the next moment might ask for something different. Adaptation isn't a destination —it's a practice, one that evolves with you as you grow, as you learn, as you become.

To dance with change is to engage fully with life's motion. It's to trust that the rhythm, even when it feels uncertain, holds something valuable. It's to believe that each step, each adjustment, each moment of alignment is part of a larger process of becoming. And as you move within the dance, you begin to see that flexibility isn't just about responding to change—it's about creating with it, shaping it, letting it shape you in return.

Chapter 4: The Energy of Tension
Section A: Tension as a Creative Force

Harnessing the Pull

Tension is often misunderstood. It's seen as something to resolve, something to overcome, something to eliminate. It pulls at you, stretches you, creates discomfort that feels unbearable at times. But tension isn't the problem—it's the energy that drives transformation. It's the force that pushes you beyond what feels comfortable, into the spaces where growth becomes possible.

At its core, tension is about potential. It's the dynamic interaction between opposites, between what is and what could be, between what you know and what you're still discovering. This pull creates energy, not just the kind that feels chaotic, but the kind that sparks motion, innovation, and change. Tension doesn't exist to tear you apart—it exists to expand you.

To harness the energy of tension is to stop fighting it and start working with it. It's to recognize that the discomfort you feel isn't something to escape—it's something to explore. What is this tension pulling you toward? What is it asking you to let go of, to lean into, to create? The energy of tension isn't about conflict— it's about connection. It's the force that bridges the gap between where you are and where you're going.

But harnessing tension requires a shift in perspective. Instead of seeing it as something negative, something to resolve as quickly as possible, you begin to see it as a teacher. Tension shows you where alignment is missing, where boundaries need to be set, where values need to be clarified. It asks you to pay attention, to notice the patterns, to feel the pull instead of resisting it. The energy of tension isn't destructive—it's instructive.

To live with tension is to live with possibility. It's to understand that the pull you feel isn't taking you away from yourself —it's guiding you toward something deeper, something truer, something more aligned. The energy of tension is the energy of creation, and when you learn to work with it, you begin to see that the discomfort isn't the end of the story—it's the beginning.

Building with Tension

Tension is not just a force to harness—it's a foundation to build upon. The pull between opposites, the discomfort of the in-between, the stretch of being asked to hold more than one truth at once—these aren't barriers to growth. They're the scaffolding that supports it. When you stop seeing tension as something to escape and start seeing it as something to work with, it becomes a powerful tool for creation.

Building with tension means acknowledging that it isn't going away. The push and pull between what is and what could be, between the familiar and the unknown, between the forces that shape your life—these are constants. They don't resolve themselves into a single, stable answer. They remain, dynamic and alive, asking you to engage with them, to shape them, to create from them. This is where the energy of tension becomes transformative.

Creation doesn't happen in a vacuum. It happens in the friction between ideas, between desires, between the present and the future. Tension sparks the imagination, forcing you to think beyond the boundaries of what you've known. It challenges you to find connections where none seem to exist, to build bridges between the opposites that pull at you. The discomfort of tension isn't a sign of failure—it's a sign of possibility.

But building with tension requires patience. The creative energy of tension doesn't unfold all at once. It asks you to sit with the discomfort, to explore the edges, to let the tension teach you what it's holding. It's in the pause, the reflection, the willingness to stay with the pull, that the new begins to emerge. Building with tension isn't about forcing solutions—it's about allowing them to take shape.

This process also requires trust. Trust that the tension has something valuable to offer, even when it feels overwhelming. Trust that the discomfort you feel is leading you toward something meaningful. Trust that the pieces you're working with —the opposites, the contradictions, the unanswered questions —are not incompatible, but complementary. The tension isn't tearing you apart—it's creating space for something new to be built.

When you build with tension, you begin to see it not as a problem to be solved, but as a resource to be used. You stop fearing the pull and start leaning into it, letting it guide you toward the insights, the connections, the growth it's asking for. The tension doesn't disappear—it transforms. It becomes the foundation for alignment, the energy for motion, the spark for creation.

To build with tension is to embrace its complexity. It's to understand that the stretch, the pull, the discomfort are not obstacles—they're invitations. They're asking you to step into the creative process, to trust the rhythm of the tension, to let it shape you as you shape it. The energy of tension is the energy of becoming, and when you build with it, you're not just navigating the pull—you're creating the harmony that emerges from it.

Section B: Reframing Discomfort
The Hidden Lessons of Pain

Discomfort often feels like a signal to stop. It's the body's way of telling you that something isn't right, that something needs to change. But not all discomfort is dangerous. Some discomfort, the kind that comes from tension and growth, isn't a warning—it's an invitation. It asks you to stay with it, to explore it, to discover the lessons it holds. Discomfort doesn't exist to push you away—it exists to pull you deeper.

At first, discomfort can feel overwhelming. It tightens your chest, quickens your breath, and tells you to retreat to what feels safer, simpler, less exposed. But discomfort doesn't arise randomly—it arises where something unresolved is asking for your attention. It's the friction between your current reality and the growth that's calling you forward. To reframe discomfort is to see it not as a threat, but as a signpost. It's pointing to the places where transformation is waiting to happen.

This reframing begins with curiosity. Instead of resisting discomfort, what happens when you lean into it? Instead of pushing it away, what happens when you ask: *Why is this here? What is this tension trying to show me? What is this pain asking me to notice?* These questions don't eliminate the discomfort, but they create space for understanding, for insight, for movement. The discomfort doesn't disappear—it transforms.

Pain has layers, and not all of them are about suffering. Sometimes pain is the weight of change, the stretch of stepping into something new, the strain of holding a truth you haven't fully embraced yet. These aren't signs that you're on the wrong path— they're signs that you're on a path that matters. Growth doesn't happen in comfort. It happens in the moments when you feel the stretch, the pull, the challenge of moving beyond what you've known.

To reframe discomfort is to see it as part of the process, not an obstacle to it. It's to trust that the tension you feel is not trying to hurt you—it's trying to teach you. And when you begin to listen to what the discomfort is saying, you begin to find the clarity, the strength, and the courage that it's been holding for you all along.

Turning Pain Into Purpose

Discomfort often feels like a wall—an immovable obstacle standing between you and the life you want to live. It tells you to stop, to turn around, to retreat to what feels easier, safer, more familiar. But discomfort isn't a wall—it's a doorway. It's the threshold between where you've been and where you're going, between what you know and what you're ready to discover. Pain, when reframed, isn't a barrier—it's a bridge.

To turn pain into purpose is to see it not as something to endure, but as something to engage with. The discomfort you feel is not random; it's connected to the places within you that are asking for change, for attention, for growth. It's the signal that something important is happening, that something within you is shifting, expanding, becoming. Discomfort is not a punishment—it's a message.

This message doesn't always arrive clearly. Pain speaks in fragments, in feelings, in moments of tension that don't immediately make sense. But when you stop resisting it, when you pause long enough to listen, you begin to hear what it's been trying to tell you all along. What are you holding onto that no longer serves you? What truths have you been avoiding because they feel too big, too heavy, too real? What would it mean to step through the discomfort instead of stepping away from it?

Turning pain into purpose doesn't mean glorifying it. It doesn't mean pretending that the discomfort isn't hard or that the tension doesn't hurt. It means recognizing that pain has a role to play in your journey, not as something to fear, but as something to learn from. Pain shows you where your values are strongest, where your boundaries need attention, where your dreams are asking to be protected. It points to the places within you that are ready to grow.

Growth isn't gentle. It stretches you, pulls at you, asks more of you than you think you can give. But that stretch, that pull, is what makes it meaningful. It's what gives the process its depth, its texture, its purpose. The discomfort you feel isn't here to break you—it's here to build you, to strengthen you, to deepen your understanding of who you are and what you're capable of.

But turning pain into purpose isn't just about reflection—it's about action. The tension you feel is asking for engagement. What small step can you take toward what feels uncomfortable? What would it mean to lean into the stretch instead of resisting it? Purpose doesn't come from waiting for the discomfort to pass— it comes from stepping into it, from using its energy to move forward, from letting it guide you toward what matters most.

This process isn't easy, and it isn't quick. Pain, like growth, is a journey. It asks for patience, for presence, for a willingness to stay with it even when it feels overwhelming. But as you engage with the discomfort, as you listen to its signals and take small steps toward its lessons, you begin to see that the tension isn't just something to endure—it's something to create with. It's not just a weight—it's a resource. It's not just pain—it's purpose.

To reframe discomfort is to reclaim your power within it. It's to see that the tension, the stretch, the pull, isn't here to stop you —it's here to move you. It's the energy of transformation, the catalyst for change, the force that pushes you toward the life you're becoming. And when you learn to turn pain into purpose, you don't just navigate the discomfort—you transcend it.

Chapter 5: The Path of Recalibration
Section A: Finding Your Balance

Stability in Motion

Balance is often imagined as a state of perfect stillness—a point where everything aligns, where the competing forces of life cancel each other out, leaving you steady, grounded, unshakable. But true balance isn't still—it's dynamic. It's not a single moment of equilibrium but a process of constant recalibration, a dance between stability and motion, clarity and chaos, presence and possibility. Balance isn't the absence of movement—it's the ability to move with intention.

To find balance in motion is to recognize that life never stops shifting. The demands placed on you, the emotions that rise and fall, the changes that shape your days—they all create a rhythm, a push and pull that keeps you in motion. This motion isn't a problem to solve—it's the rhythm of being alive. Balance isn't about stopping the movement—it's about learning to flow with it, to adjust, to recalibrate as the rhythm changes.

Recalibration begins with awareness. What forces are at play in your life right now? What's pulling you forward, and what's holding you back? Where do you feel grounded, and where do you feel untethered? Balance isn't something you achieve once and for all—it's something you create moment by moment, by noticing the shifts, the tensions, the opportunities to adjust. It's not a destination—it's a practice.

This practice doesn't ask for perfection. It doesn't require you to hold every piece of your life in perfect alignment at all times. It asks for presence. It asks you to notice when you're leaning too far in one direction, when the weight of one responsibility or one emotion or one relationship begins to pull you off center. And it asks you to respond, to adjust, to shift your weight and find your footing again.

To find your balance is not to erase the forces that pull at you—it's to integrate them. The push of one responsibility, the pull of another, the sway of your own emotions and needs—they're not competing forces. They're part of the same rhythm, and balance comes not from eliminating them but from learning how to move with them. It's about recognizing that the forces in your life are not here to destabilize you—they're here to teach you how to adapt, how to recalibrate, how to create harmony within motion.

This process of recalibration isn't a chore—it's a creative act. It's the art of adjusting, of finding the patterns within the push and pull, of discovering the rhythm that allows you to feel steady even when everything around you is in motion. Balance doesn't mean the absence of tension—it means the ability to work with it, to turn the pull of competing forces into the energy that keeps you moving forward.

To find stability in motion is to trust yourself. It's to believe that even when the rhythm feels chaotic, you have the ability to recalibrate, to adjust, to create balance within the flux. It's to see balance not as something you achieve once but as something you practice again and again, creating harmony not in the stillness, but in the movement.

The Practice of Alignment

Balance isn't something you find and hold forever. It's something you create and recreate, moment by moment. The forces that shape your life are always in motion, and balance requires you to move with them, to adjust as they change, to recalibrate as new challenges and opportunities arise. It's not about perfect alignment—it's about practicing alignment, over and over again.

The practice of alignment begins with listening. Balance isn't about forcing everything into place—it's about noticing what feels out of place. Where do you feel tension? What feels heavy? What feels neglected? These questions don't offer immediate solutions, but they open the door to awareness, to understanding the dynamics at play in your life. Balance starts with knowing where you are before deciding where to go.

From this awareness, you can begin to shift. Recalibration doesn't require grand gestures or sweeping changes—it begins with small, intentional adjustments. It's the act of noticing when something feels unsteady and choosing to engage with it. Maybe it's taking a moment to breathe when you feel overwhelmed. Maybe it's setting a boundary where none existed before. Maybe it's letting go of something you've been holding onto too tightly. Recalibration isn't about fixing everything—it's about finding your footing in the moment you're in.

But alignment isn't just about external adjustments—it's about internal clarity. To recalibrate, you need to know what you're aligning with. What are your values? What matters most to you right now? What do you need to let go of to make space for what feels true? The practice of alignment isn't about achieving perfection—it's about staying connected to what's meaningful, even as the circumstances around you shift.

Recalibration also requires compassion. Balance isn't something you get right all the time, and that's OK. There will be moments when the pull of life feels too strong, when the tension feels too heavy, when the rhythm feels impossible to follow. In these moments, the practice isn't about judgment—it's about grace. It's about giving yourself permission to stumble, to lose your balance, to pause and regroup. The path of recalibration isn't linear—it's cyclical. And every time you return to it, you strengthen your ability to adapt.

To live within the practice of alignment is to embrace life's motion. It's to see balance not as an endpoint, but as a dynamic process, a rhythm that you create and recreate as you move through the flux of existence. It's to trust that even when the ground feels unsteady, you have the capacity to find your center, to adjust, to move forward with intention. Recalibration isn't a single act—it's a way of being. And with each adjustment, you don't just find your balance—you deepen your connection to yourself and the life you're creating.

Section B: The Art of the Pivot
Responding to the Shift

Life rarely unfolds the way we expect. Plans falter, circumstances change, and the paths we thought were certain suddenly shift beneath our feet. In these moments, the ability to pivot becomes essential—not as a sign of failure or indecision, but as an act of adaptability, a way of honoring the new reality while staying connected to what matters most. The pivot isn't about abandoning your direction—it's about finding a new way forward.

To pivot is to respond, not react. It's the act of pausing when the ground shifts, of noticing the new landscape, and asking: *What is this moment asking of me? What adjustments can I make to align with this change rather than resisting it?* The pivot doesn't erase the motion—it works with it, turning what feels like an obstacle into an opportunity to recalibrate, to reimagine, to continue moving forward.

Responding to the shift begins with presence. When change disrupts your plans, it's natural to feel a surge of frustration, fear, or resistance. The instinct is to push back, to try to force the world to conform to your expectations. But the pivot asks for a different response. It asks you to pause, to breathe, to notice the shift without judgment. What has changed? What hasn't? What possibilities does this new reality hold, even if it feels uncertain or uncomfortable?

The pivot also asks for flexibility—not just in your actions, but in your mindset. It's the willingness to let go of the idea that there's only one "right" way forward, and to embrace the idea that the new path might hold something valuable, something you couldn't have seen before. Flexibility doesn't mean giving up—it means opening up, expanding your perspective to include the possibilities that exist in the shift.

But the pivot isn't just about moving—it's about moving with intention. When you respond to the shift, you're not abandoning your values or your goals—you're finding a new way to align with them. The pivot asks you to reconnect with what matters most, to let your values guide your next step, even if that step looks different than the one you originally planned. The shift doesn't mean you've lost your direction—it means you're discovering a new one.

To pivot is to trust the process. It's to believe that even when the path changes, the journey continues. It's to see the shift not as a detour, but as part of the rhythm of becoming. The pivot isn't just a reaction to change—it's a choice to engage with it, to move with it, to create something meaningful within it. And in that choice, you find your way forward.

Reimagining the Path

To pivot is not just to respond to change—it's to reimagine what's possible. When the ground shifts beneath you, when the plans you carefully crafted unravel, the instinct is often to cling to what was, to try to force your way back to the path you thought you were on. But the art of the pivot isn't about going back—it's about stepping into what comes next. It's about seeing the shift not as the end of the story, but as the beginning of a new chapter.

Reimagining the path begins with letting go of what no longer serves you. This isn't about giving up—it's about recognizing that the path you were on was tied to a set of circumstances that may no longer exist. It's about asking yourself: *What am I holding onto that's keeping me stuck? What would it mean to release this, to open myself to a new possibility?* Letting go is not a loss—it's a transformation. It creates the space for something new to take shape.

This new shape often emerges slowly, piece by piece. The pivot doesn't require you to see the entire path at once—it asks you to trust the process of discovery. What feels true in this moment? What small step can you take toward alignment? What new opportunities are revealed when you stop looking for the path you lost and start noticing the one that's forming in front of you? The pivot is an act of creation, a way of building the path as you walk it.

Reimagining the path also asks you to embrace uncertainty. The pivot doesn't promise clarity—it promises motion. It invites you to step forward even when the destination isn't fully visible, to trust that the act of moving will bring new insights, new connections, new possibilities. Uncertainty isn't something to resolve—it's something to live within, a space where creativity and courage intersect to create something new.

But the pivot isn't just about external change—it's about internal alignment. It's about asking yourself: *What do I value most in this moment? How can I move in a way that reflects those values, even in the midst of uncertainty? What would it look like to honor what matters to me, even if the path looks different than I expected?* The pivot is an act of integrity, a way of staying true to yourself even as the world around you changes.

To pivot is to engage fully with life's motion. It's to see the shifts, the disruptions, the unexpected turns not as obstacles, but as invitations to grow, to adapt, to create. It's to trust that the path you're on is always evolving, always revealing itself, one step at a time. The pivot isn't a detour—it's a practice, a way of living within the rhythm of change, of becoming.

Chapter 6: The Freedom in Impermanence
Section A: Letting Go of Permanence
The Illusion of Forever

We crave permanence. It promises safety, stability, and the comforting idea that once something is achieved, it will stay exactly as it is. We build plans, relationships, and identities around the hope that they will last unchanged, offering us a sense of certainty in a world that feels unpredictable. But permanence is an illusion. Life is not static—it is in motion, always shifting, always evolving. To hold onto the idea of forever is to resist the very nature of existence.

Letting go of permanence isn't about giving up hope or abandoning your dreams—it's about freeing yourself from the weight of expectations that life will stay the same. It's about recognizing that everything—your experiences, your relationships, your successes, your struggles—is part of a larger rhythm, one that flows with the currents of time and change. Impermanence isn't a flaw in the system—it's the system itself.

At first, this idea can feel unsettling. To acknowledge impermanence is to acknowledge that nothing is guaranteed, that the things you hold most dear will inevitably change. But impermanence isn't just about loss—it's about transformation. It reminds you that nothing stays the same, but everything has the potential to grow, to evolve, to become something new. The freedom in impermanence lies in this possibility: that what changes is not gone, but transformed.

Letting go of permanence also means letting go of the fear of change. The idea of forever can create a false sense of control, a belief that if you just hold on tightly enough, you can prevent the shifts that feel uncomfortable or uncertain. But the tighter you hold, the more you resist the natural flow of life. To let go of permanence is to stop clinging to what was and to open yourself to what is. It's to trust that change, as disruptive as it feels, carries with it the seeds of renewal.

This isn't about denying the pain of impermanence. Change often brings loss, and loss is hard. It asks you to release things you weren't ready to let go of, to step into spaces you don't yet understand. But within that pain lies the opportunity for growth, for discovery, for a deeper connection to the rhythm of life itself. To let go of permanence is not to deny your grief—it's to honor it as part of the process of becoming.

The illusion of forever is comforting, but it limits you. It keeps you tied to a static vision of what life should be, rather than allowing you to engage with what life is. Letting go of that illusion doesn't mean letting go of hope—it means shifting your focus from what you want to preserve to what you want to create. Impermanence isn't a loss—it's a freedom, a reminder that life is always unfolding, always offering new possibilities, always inviting you to grow.

The Flow of Release

Letting go is an act of courage. It's a choice to trust the flow of life even when it asks you to release what you thought you couldn't live without. The idea of permanence convinces you that holding on is strength, that clinging to what feels familiar is the safest way forward. But the truth is, life's motion doesn't stop for anyone. To live fully is to let go, not as an act of surrender, but as an act of trust—trust that the flow will carry you, even as it transforms what you leave behind.

Release isn't about forgetting or abandoning—it's about making space. When you hold onto something too tightly, you close yourself off to what could be. You limit your capacity to grow, to discover, to create. Letting go doesn't erase what came before— it honors it, recognizing that its role in your life has changed. It allows you to carry forward the meaning, the lessons, the essence of what mattered, without being bound by the need to keep it exactly as it was.

This flow of release is not passive. It's an active engagement with the rhythm of impermanence, a willingness to feel the grief, the uncertainty, the vulnerability that comes with change. To let go is to step into the unknown, to move with life's currents instead of resisting them. It's to understand that holding on too tightly doesn't preserve what matters—it distorts it, turning what once brought joy into a source of tension, what once felt alive into something static.

Letting go also means letting yourself evolve. Just as the external world changes, so do you. The dreams you held ten years ago may no longer align with who you are today. The relationships that once felt essential may no longer feel like home. The routines that grounded you may now feel like constraints. Letting go of permanence isn't just about releasing external attachments— it's about allowing yourself the freedom to grow, to change, to become.

This doesn't mean the process is easy. Letting go often feels like loss, and loss carries grief. It's important to honor that grief, to allow yourself to feel it fully without rushing to move past it. But within that grief lies a quiet truth: that every ending carries the seed of a beginning. To release what no longer serves you is to open yourself to what comes next, to create space for new experiences, new connections, new possibilities.

The flow of release isn't a single act—it's a practice. It's a way of living that embraces impermanence not as something to fear, but as something to trust. It's the recognition that life's motion isn't taking things from you—it's carrying you forward. To let go is to join that motion, to move with it, to allow it to shape you into the person you are becoming.

Section B: Embracing the Temporary
Joy in the Moment

Impermanence carries with it a quiet gift: the reminder to find joy in the fleeting moments of life. When nothing is guaranteed to last, each experience, each connection, each breath becomes more precious. The awareness of impermanence invites you to be fully present, to savor the beauty of what is, without clinging to the need for it to remain the same.

Joy in the moment isn't about ignoring the reality of change—it's about embracing it. It's about seeing the temporary nature of life not as a loss but as an invitation. The things you love, the experiences that shape you, the people you hold dear—they matter not despite their impermanence, but because of it. Their transience gives them depth, meaning, and a sense of urgency to be fully engaged with, here and now.

This kind of joy doesn't come from pretending that the temporary won't end. It comes from choosing to immerse yourself in the experience while it's here, knowing that its impermanence doesn't diminish its value. It's the smile of a child that will soon grow older, the warmth of a conversation that may not happen again, the quiet peace of a moment that will soon shift into something new. These are not things to fear losing—they are things to cherish while they last.

To embrace the temporary is to honor the flow of life. It's to understand that every ending carries with it the possibility of a new beginning, that what feels fleeting is part of a larger rhythm, a constant process of renewal and transformation. The temporary isn't something to fix or hold onto—it's something to live within, to feel deeply, to celebrate even as it changes.

Joy in impermanence also teaches you to let go of perfection. When you stop clinging to the idea that things must last forever to have meaning, you free yourself to appreciate them for what they are. The messy, imperfect, fleeting moments of life hold their own kind of beauty, a beauty that exists not in their permanence but in their aliveness. To embrace the temporary is to see that life's motion isn't taking something away from you—it's giving you the chance to experience it fully, even if only for a moment.

This joy isn't about denying the grief that comes with change. It's about holding that grief alongside the gratitude, about letting the sorrow of impermanence deepen your appreciation for what was and what is. It's about seeing the temporary not as a limitation but as a reminder to live more fully, to love more deeply, to engage more authentically with the moments you have.

Living Lightly

To embrace the temporary is to learn how to live lightly—not in the sense of being carefree or detached, but in the sense of moving through life with openness, grace, and an awareness of its fleeting nature. Living lightly means carrying the moments of joy, the lessons of pain, and the connections that shape you without letting them weigh you down. It means holding life not with clenched fists, but with open hands.

Impermanence invites you to live lightly because it shows you that nothing can be held forever. The people you love, the dreams you chase, the stability you create—all of it will change, will shift, will transform. To live lightly is to carry these truths without resistance, to let them deepen your presence rather than burden your heart. It's to recognize that impermanence doesn't diminish what matters—it illuminates it.

Living lightly doesn't mean living without care. It means living with intention. It means choosing to engage deeply with the moments and connections that feel meaningful, while letting go of the need to control or preserve them. It's about being fully present with what is, rather than clinging to what was or worrying about what will be. It's about trusting that life's motion will carry you, even when you don't know where it's taking you.

To live lightly is also to release the weight of expectations. Impermanence reminds you that life rarely unfolds exactly as planned, and that's not a flaw—it's a feature. When you let go of the need for certainty, for permanence, for perfection, you create space for something new to emerge. You create space for possibility, for creativity, for the unexpected beauty that can only come when you stop trying to hold everything in place.

But living lightly doesn't mean avoiding the depth of life's experiences. It's not about floating above the pain or sidestepping the grief that comes with change. It's about being fully present with those emotions, allowing them to move through you, and trusting that they, too, are part of the rhythm of impermanence. Living lightly means carrying the weight of life without letting it crush you. It means finding strength in your openness, resilience in your ability to let go.

To embrace the temporary is to embrace the freedom of living lightly. It's to see that life isn't about accumulating moments to hold onto—it's about experiencing them fully, letting them shape you, and allowing them to flow through you as part of the larger motion of becoming. It's about trusting that even as things change, even as you release what you once thought you couldn't live without, you are always moving forward, always growing, always creating something new.

Chapter 7: The Spiral of Growth
Section A: Cycles Within Cycles

Returning to Move Forward

Growth isn't linear. It doesn't unfold as a straight path leading neatly from one point to another. Instead, it moves in spirals, circling back to familiar places, revisiting old themes, returning to what you thought you'd left behind. At first, this can feel frustrating, even discouraging. *Why am I back here? Haven't I already dealt with this?* But the spiral doesn't bring you back to the same place—it brings you back with new depth, new perspective, new understanding.

The spiral of growth isn't a repetition—it's an evolution. Each time you circle back, you're not the same person you were before. The experiences you've had, the lessons you've learned, the challenges you've faced—they've all shaped you, deepened you, prepared you to engage with what you're revisiting in a different way. The spiral doesn't ask you to start over—it invites you to move forward by moving deeper.

Returning to familiar struggles, familiar patterns, familiar questions is part of the process of becoming. It's a reminder that growth is not about leaving your past behind—it's about integrating it, learning from it, using it to inform your next steps. The themes you revisit aren't signs of failure—they're opportunities to see how far you've come, to engage with them from a place of greater awareness and strength.

To embrace the spiral is to let go of the idea that growth should be linear. It's to accept that progress often looks like circling back, revisiting, recalibrating. The spiral isn't a detour—it's the path itself. And each loop, each return, brings you closer to alignment, closer to a deeper understanding of who you are and what you're becoming.

Growth Through Returning

When the spiral brings you back to a place you've been before, it can feel disheartening, as though the progress you've made has been erased. You find yourself facing the same questions, the same struggles, the same patterns that you thought you'd left behind. But growth isn't about escaping these returns—it's about engaging with them more deeply each time they appear. The spiral doesn't repeat—it evolves. And with every turn, it carries you closer to a fuller understanding of yourself.

Growth through returning is about perspective. The struggles you face today may look similar to the ones you faced before, but you are not the same. The lessons you've learned, the resilience you've built, the insights you've gained—they all shape how you approach what's in front of you now. You're not starting over—you're building on what came before. The spiral reminds you that growth isn't about avoiding challenges—it's about meeting them with new tools, new awareness, new strength.

Returning to old themes isn't a sign of failure—it's a sign of depth. The spiral of growth moves in cycles, each one building on the last, each one inviting you to explore a familiar place from a new perspective. What feels like repetition is often transformation in disguise. The questions you're asking now may echo the ones you asked before, but the answers you're seeking have changed because you've changed. The spiral brings you back not to hold you in place, but to show you how far you've come.

But growth through returning isn't just about reflection—it's about engagement. The spiral doesn't move on its own—it moves with you, inviting you to take action, to lean into the lessons it's offering. What can you do differently this time? What have you learned from the last time you faced this challenge? What new steps can you take to align more fully with who you are becoming? The spiral asks you to be an active participant in your growth, to use each return as an opportunity to refine, to recalibrate, to move forward.

This forward motion isn't always obvious. The spiral doesn't unfold in straight lines or predictable patterns. It loops, it doubles back, it twists and turns, often in ways that feel confusing or frustrating. But each loop brings you closer to alignment, each turn reveals new possibilities, each return deepens your understanding. The spiral of growth isn't about reaching a final destination—it's about becoming more of who you are, step by step, cycle by cycle.

To grow through returning is to trust the process. It's to believe that even when it feels like you're back where you started, you're not the same. The spiral carries you forward, not by avoiding the past, but by integrating it. And with each loop, with each return, you find not just who you've been, but who you're becoming.

Section B: Progress in Reflection
Revisiting to Move Forward

Reflection isn't about dwelling on the past—it's about using the past to understand the present and shape the future. When you revisit the cycles of your life, the challenges you've faced, the choices you've made, it's not an act of reliving—it's an act of learning. Progress doesn't come from leaving the past behind—it comes from carrying it with you, not as a weight, but as a resource, a guide, a foundation for what's next.

To revisit is to ask questions: *What brought me here? What patterns do I see? What lessons have I learned that I can apply now?* These questions don't bind you to the past—they free you to move forward with greater clarity and intention. They remind you that your journey isn't about starting from scratch—it's about building on what you've already discovered, about using what you've learned to navigate the next cycle with more awareness, more grace, more purpose.

Reflection reveals progress that isn't always visible in the moment. When you're in the midst of growth, it's easy to feel like you're not moving, like the steps you're taking aren't adding up to anything meaningful. But when you step back and look at the larger pattern, you begin to see how far you've come. The challenges that once felt insurmountable now feel manageable. The questions that once felt unanswerable now hold insights you couldn't have imagined before. Reflection shows you that progress isn't always about leaps—it's about the steady, quiet movement that happens over time.

But progress in reflection isn't just about looking back—it's about looking forward. The spiral of growth asks you to use the lessons of the past to shape the choices you make in the present, to align your actions with the values and goals that have become clearer through reflection. What do you want to carry forward? What do you want to leave behind? What new possibilities are revealed when you let the past inform, but not dictate, your next steps?

To revisit is not to repeat—it's to refine. The spiral of growth brings you back not to hold you in place, but to show you how far you've come, to remind you that the work you've done has value, and to invite you to use that work as a foundation for what comes next. Progress isn't about perfection—it's about engagement. And with each cycle, each reflection, you move closer to the alignment, the authenticity, the becoming that you seek.

Building Forward

Reflection isn't just about understanding where you've been—it's about building on it, carrying its lessons into the present to create something meaningful in the future. Progress through reflection isn't a static process; it's active, dynamic, and deeply creative. It asks you to engage with your past not as something fixed, but as a resource—a foundation for the choices you're making now and the paths you're forging ahead.

Building forward begins with recognizing the threads of continuity in your journey. The challenges you've faced, the moments of clarity you've found, the patterns you've uncovered —these are not isolated events. They are part of a larger story, a narrative that is still unfolding. Reflection allows you to trace these threads, to see how they've shaped who you are, and to weave them into the fabric of who you're becoming.

But building forward also requires discernment. Not everything you've carried with you needs to come along for the next phase of the journey. Reflection asks you to sift through your experiences, your habits, your beliefs, and to ask: *What still serves me? What no longer aligns with who I am or who I want to be? What do I need to release to create space for what's next?* Progress isn't just about adding—it's about letting go, about refining, about choosing what matters most.

The act of building forward is an act of creation. It's not about recreating the past or adhering to a fixed plan—it's about using the materials of your experience to shape something new. It's about seeing the lessons you've learned not as endpoints, but as stepping stones. What insights have you gained that can inform your next decision? What strengths have you developed that can support you in the challenges ahead? What values have become clearer through reflection, and how can they guide the path you're creating?

Progress through reflection isn't linear—it loops, spirals, and overlaps. The questions you ask today may lead to answers that open new questions tomorrow. The insights you uncover may not fully reveal their meaning until you revisit them later, in a different context, from a new perspective. This isn't a flaw in the process—it's the process itself. Growth is recursive, building layer upon layer, cycle upon cycle, creating depth and texture as it evolves.

To build forward is to trust this process. It's to believe that the work you're doing now—the reflection, the questioning, the small steps you're taking—is part of something larger, something meaningful, even if you can't see the full picture yet. It's to recognize that progress isn't about reaching a final destination—it's about engaging fully with the journey, about letting each step, each cycle, each reflection bring you closer to alignment.

Building forward isn't about erasing the past—it's about transforming it. It's about carrying its wisdom, its lessons, its truths into the present, using them to create a future that feels authentic, aligned, and alive. The spiral of growth doesn't just bring you back to what you've known—it carries you forward, inviting you to use what you've learned to create something new. And with each turn, each reflection, each act of building, you become more of who you are meant to be.

Chapter 8: The Rhythm of Relationships

Section A: Connection in Motion

Relationships as Living Systems

Relationships are not static—they are living, breathing systems, constantly evolving as the people within them grow, change, and navigate the complexities of life. Like all living things, relationships thrive on care, attention, and adaptability. They require nurturing, recalibration, and a willingness to move with their rhythm rather than trying to hold them in place. To connect deeply with others is to step into this dynamic motion, to engage with relationships as processes, not as fixed states.

The dynamic nature of relationships can feel both exhilarating and unsettling. On one hand, it creates opportunities for growth, discovery, and transformation. On the other, it challenges you to let go of the illusion that any connection can stay exactly the same forever. Relationships, like the individuals within them, are always in motion. They change shape, evolve in purpose, and sometimes reach natural endings. To embrace the rhythm of relationships is to honor this motion, to see it not as a threat but as the very thing that keeps connection alive.

At their core, relationships are about exchange—the exchange of energy, ideas, emotions, and experiences. This exchange is what creates the rhythm, the give-and-take that allows relationships to flourish. But for this rhythm to remain healthy, it must be balanced. Too much giving without receiving leads to depletion. Too much taking without giving leads to disconnection. The rhythm isn't about keeping score—it's about creating harmony, a flow that feels mutually supportive and nourishing.

Connection in motion also requires presence. Relationships are not sustained by past memories or future hopes—they are sustained by how you show up in the present moment. What does this person need from you right now? What do you need from them? How can you engage with the relationship as it exists today, not as you wish it would be or fear it might become? The rhythm of connection is found in these moments of presence, where you choose to meet the other person where they are and allow them to meet you where you are.

This motion isn't always smooth. Relationships, like any living system, experience friction, tension, and periods of imbalance. But these moments are not failures—they are opportunities to recalibrate, to adjust the rhythm, to deepen the connection. To navigate relationships in motion is to accept that tension is part of the process, that it holds within it the energy for growth and the potential for greater understanding.

To connect deeply is to move with the rhythm of relationships, to see them not as static entities but as dynamic exchanges. It's to embrace the motion, the shifts, the transformations that make them alive. And as you engage with this rhythm, you discover that connection isn't something you achieve—it's something you create, moment by moment, step by step, together.

Navigating Shifts Together

Relationships are journeys shared by individuals who are themselves always in motion. As you grow, learn, and change, so too do your connections with others. The rhythm of a relationship isn't a constant—it evolves, shifts, and sometimes stumbles. Navigating these shifts isn't about resisting the changes or clinging to what was—it's about moving together, finding alignment within the motion, and allowing the connection to grow with you.

Navigating shifts begins with understanding that relationships are not one-sided. They are collaborations, partnerships in which each person's needs, boundaries, and growth are equally important. When the rhythm changes—when a relationship feels out of sync or tension arises—it's often a signal that one or both people have shifted in ways that need attention. These moments aren't failures—they're invitations to adjust, to reconnect, to recalibrate the rhythm you share.

To move through these shifts together, you must be willing to communicate openly and honestly. What has changed? What do you need from each other now that might be different from what you needed before? What tensions are arising, and how can they be addressed with curiosity instead of blame? These conversations can feel vulnerable, but vulnerability is what creates the space for connection to deepen. It's what allows you to see and be seen, not as static versions of yourselves, but as evolving, dynamic individuals.

Navigating shifts also requires flexibility. The rhythm of a relationship will never stay the same, and that's not a sign of instability—it's a sign of life. Flexibility means being willing to adapt to the changes in your own needs and in the needs of the other person. It means letting go of rigid expectations about how the relationship should look and embracing the reality of what it is. Flexibility isn't about sacrificing yourself—it's about creating space for both people to grow, together and individually.

But moving through shifts isn't just about accommodating change—it's about celebrating it. Change within a relationship is a sign that the connection is alive, that it has the capacity to evolve rather than stagnate. It's a sign that the relationship is not something to preserve in amber but something to nurture, to shape, to co-create. When you celebrate the shifts, you stop seeing them as disruptions and start seeing them as opportunities—for growth, for renewal, for deeper connection.

This process isn't always easy. There will be moments when the rhythm feels hard to find, when the changes feel too big, when the tension feels overwhelming. But these moments are part of the journey. They ask you to engage with the relationship fully, to bring your presence, your curiosity, your willingness to move with the motion rather than resist it. The rhythm may falter, but it can always be found again—together.

To navigate shifts in relationships is to embrace their motion, to see the changes not as threats but as opportunities to grow closer, to understand each other more deeply, to build something that reflects who you are now. Relationships aren't static—they are alive, dynamic, and always becoming. And when you move through their rhythms with openness and care, you discover that connection isn't about holding on—it's about moving forward, side by side.

Section B: Navigating Together
Honoring Each Other's Rhythms

Relationships are not a single rhythm—they are the interplay of two or more. Each person brings their own tempo, their own cadence, their own needs and desires to the connection. At times, these rhythms align perfectly, creating a sense of harmony that feels effortless. But more often, relationships require negotiation, adjustment, and a willingness to honor each other's rhythms, even when they differ from your own.

Honoring another's rhythm begins with listening. It's not about assuming what the other person needs or trying to impose your own expectations—it's about being present enough to hear what they're asking for, whether through words, actions, or the silences in between. What tempo is this person moving at right now? Do they need space, or do they need closeness? Are they surging forward, or are they in a moment of retreat? Listening isn't just an act of kindness—it's an act of connection.

But listening alone isn't enough. To honor another's rhythm, you must also be willing to adapt, to adjust your own tempo in ways that create alignment without losing yourself. This doesn't mean sacrificing your needs or abandoning your own rhythm—it means finding the overlaps, the spaces where your tempos can coexist. It's about creating a dynamic balance, a shared rhythm that allows both of you to move together without one person's pace overwhelming the other's.

This balance isn't static—it's fluid. There will be times when your rhythms naturally align, when the connection feels effortless and smooth. And there will be times when they clash, when the tempo of one person feels too fast or too slow for the other. These moments of dissonance aren't failures—they're opportunities to recalibrate, to communicate, to find a new rhythm that works for where you both are now.

To navigate together is also to acknowledge that your rhythms won't always be in sync, and that's OK. Relationships aren't about perfect alignment at all times—they're about mutual respect, about holding space for each other's differences while still moving toward a shared connection. It's about learning when to step forward and when to step back, when to match the other person's pace and when to hold steady in your own.

Honoring each other's rhythms requires patience, flexibility, and a willingness to engage with the relationship as a living, evolving process. It's not about fixing the moments when the rhythms feel off—it's about staying present with them, about trusting that the motion itself will bring you back into alignment. The dance of relationships isn't always graceful, but it is always an opportunity to grow—together.

Growing Through Connection

Relationships are not just about harmony—they're about growth. The rhythm you share with another person isn't static; it evolves as you both evolve. Navigating together means accepting that your connection will face moments of alignment and misalignment, ease and tension, flow and friction. These moments aren't obstacles—they're opportunities to deepen your connection, to learn from each other, and to grow both as individuals and as a pair.

Growth through connection begins with a willingness to be vulnerable. To truly navigate together, you must be willing to show up fully—not just with your strengths, but with your uncertainties, your fears, your questions. Vulnerability isn't weakness; it's the openness that allows relationships to thrive. When you let yourself be seen, you create space for the other person to do the same, building a rhythm of trust that carries you through the challenges and changes you face.

But growth also requires tension. Relationships, like any dynamic system, need energy to stay alive, and tension is one of the forces that creates that energy. Disagreements, misunderstandings, and moments of disconnection are not failures—they are the sparks that push you to explore each other's needs, to clarify your boundaries, to deepen your understanding of what the connection means. The tension isn't something to fear—it's something to work with, something to transform into a deeper sense of alignment.

Navigating together also means recognizing that growth doesn't always happen at the same pace. There will be times when one person moves forward while the other holds back, times when one person's rhythm feels out of step with the other's. These moments ask for patience, for flexibility, for a commitment to holding space for each other's growth without trying to force it. Growth isn't about moving in lockstep—it's about supporting each other as you move in your own ways, trusting that the connection will find its rhythm again.

To grow through connection is to embrace the imperfections of relationships. It's to see the moments of tension not as threats but as invitations, the moments of misalignment not as problems but as opportunities to realign. It's to understand that the rhythm you share isn't about being perfectly in sync at all times—it's about staying engaged, staying curious, staying committed to the process of navigating together.

Relationships, like the individuals within them, are always becoming. They are not fixed—they are alive, dynamic, and full of possibility. To navigate together is to honor this motion, to trust that the shifts, the changes, the challenges are not taking you apart but bringing you closer, helping you to grow both as individuals and as a connection. Growth through connection isn't about reaching a final state of harmony—it's about learning to move together within the rhythm of life itself.

Chapter 9: The Power of Perspective
Section A: Shifting the Lens

Seeing Differently

Perspective shapes everything. It colors how you interpret your experiences, how you understand the people around you, how you see yourself in the world. But perspective is not fixed—it's fluid, dynamic, and open to change. The power of perspective lies in your ability to shift it, to step outside the frame of your current view and see things differently. This shift doesn't just change what you see—it changes what's possible.

Seeing differently begins with curiosity. What if the story you're telling yourself about this moment isn't the only story? What if the challenge you're facing isn't a dead end, but a turning point? What if the tension you feel isn't a problem, but a signal pointing you toward something that needs your attention? Curiosity invites you to question your assumptions, to explore the edges of your understanding, to consider perspectives you might have overlooked.

But shifting the lens isn't just about asking questions—it's about stepping into new angles of vision. Sometimes this means widening the frame, zooming out to see the bigger picture. What patterns are at play in this situation? How does this moment connect to the larger rhythm of your life? Other times, it means narrowing the focus, zooming in to notice the details you've missed. What small gestures, small shifts, small truths are hidden within this moment? The act of shifting perspective isn't about finding the "right" view—it's about discovering the many layers of meaning that exist within each experience.

Perspective is powerful because it shapes not just what you see, but how you respond. When you change the lens through which you view a challenge, you open the door to new possibilities, new solutions, new ways of engaging with the world. The problem that felt insurmountable might now feel manageable. The relationship that felt strained might now feel worth nurturing. The moment that felt heavy might now hold a glimmer of light. Perspective doesn't erase the challenges—it transforms your relationship with them.

To shift the lens is to remind yourself that your current perspective is not the only one. It's to step outside your default way of seeing and choose a different angle, a different story, a different truth. And in that shift, you don't just change what you see—you change what you believe is possible.

Changing the Story

Perspective is more than how you see the world—it's the story you tell yourself about what you see. It's the narrative that shapes your understanding of events, your relationships, your sense of self. But stories are not fixed. They can be rewritten, revised, expanded. When you change the story, you change not just how you see the world but how you experience it. Perspective has the power to transform, and that transformation begins with the stories you choose to tell.

Changing the story doesn't mean denying the reality of what's happening. It doesn't mean glossing over pain or pretending challenges don't exist. It means expanding the narrative, making space for complexity, for nuance, for possibility. What if the struggle you're facing isn't just about what's going wrong but about what's trying to emerge? What if the relationship that feels difficult isn't about failure but about an opportunity to grow closer through tension? What if the disappointment you're carrying isn't an ending but a doorway into something new?

The stories you tell yourself shape how you engage with life. A story that frames a challenge as insurmountable leads to retreat, to stagnation. A story that frames the same challenge as an opportunity leads to curiosity, to action. Changing the story isn't about dismissing the difficulty—it's about choosing to see the possibilities it holds. It's about shifting from a narrative of limitation to one of growth, from one of fear to one of courage, from one of resistance to one of engagement.

This process begins with awareness. What story are you telling yourself about this moment? Is it a story of lack, of impossibility, of defeat? Or is it a story of potential, of resilience, of becoming? The stories you default to aren't always the ones that serve you— they're often shaped by past experiences, by fears, by assumptions that no longer align with who you are. To change the story, you must first notice it, question it, and ask: *What other story could I tell?*

But rewriting the narrative isn't just about changing your thoughts—it's about changing your actions. The story you choose to tell influences the choices you make, the steps you take, the way you move through the world. A story of defeat keeps you stuck, but a story of possibility invites you to move forward, even if the path isn't clear. Changing the story isn't about ignoring the challenges—it's about seeing them as part of a larger narrative, one in which you are not just a passive participant but an active creator.

Perspective isn't static. It shifts with the stories you tell, the actions you take, the questions you ask. To change the story is to reclaim your power within it. It's to remind yourself that the narrative isn't fixed—it's alive, dynamic, and open to revision. And as you change the story, you don't just change how you see the world—you change how you engage with it, how you grow within it, how you become.

Section B: The Gift of Curiosity
Opening the Door

Curiosity is a doorway. It invites you to step beyond the limits of what you think you know, into a space where new possibilities can emerge. It's not about finding definitive answers or achieving certainty—it's about asking questions that expand your perspective, questions that challenge assumptions and create room for growth. Curiosity is the key to unlocking the potential hidden in every moment, every challenge, every connection.

The gift of curiosity begins with a willingness to wonder. What lies beyond this fear, this tension, this discomfort? What new understanding might emerge if you looked at this situation from a different angle? What could happen if you let go of needing to be right and instead allowed yourself to explore what's true? Curiosity doesn't demand resolution—it thrives in the space of not knowing, in the openness to discovery.

Curiosity isn't just about what's outside of you—it's also about what's within. What emotions are rising in this moment, and what might they be trying to tell you? What beliefs are shaping the way you see this situation, and how might those beliefs be limiting your perspective? What assumptions are you carrying, and what would it mean to set them down? To be curious about yourself is to step into a deeper relationship with who you are, to engage with the layers of your experience that often go unnoticed.

But curiosity isn't always comfortable. It asks you to sit with uncertainty, to step into the unknown, to entertain possibilities that might feel unsettling or unexpected. It challenges the stories you've told yourself, the patterns you've relied on, the truths you've clung to. But this discomfort is where curiosity does its work. It's in the questioning, the exploring, the wondering that new insights arise, that new paths become visible.

Curiosity also teaches you to approach others with openness. What is this person experiencing that I might not see? What fears or hopes are shaping their actions? What would it mean to truly listen, to set aside my assumptions and engage with their reality as it is, not as I imagine it to be? Curiosity turns judgment into understanding, creating space for connection where there was once distance.

To embrace the gift of curiosity is to embrace life as a process of becoming. It's to see every challenge, every relationship, every moment as an opportunity to learn, to expand, to deepen your understanding of the world and your place within it. Curiosity doesn't solve all the problems or answer all the questions—but it opens the door to something greater, something more meaningful, something more alive.

Expanding the Possible

Curiosity doesn't just open doors—it expands the world beyond them. It transforms the limits of what you think is possible, broadening your understanding and inviting you to see what lies beyond the familiar. When you approach life with curiosity, the edges of your perspective soften, creating room for exploration, for creativity, for growth. Curiosity reminds you that no moment, no challenge, no relationship is ever fully understood—it's always unfolding, always holding something new to discover.

Expanding the possible begins with a single question: *What else could this be?* What else could this challenge teach me? What else might this person be feeling? What else is present in this moment that I haven't yet noticed? These questions don't demand answers —they invite possibilities. They create space for you to step outside your default way of seeing and into a perspective that is broader, richer, and more dynamic.

Curiosity also requires humility. It asks you to acknowledge that your current understanding, no matter how complete it feels, is always partial. There is always more to learn, more to see, more to uncover. This isn't a flaw in your perspective—it's a feature of being human. To be curious is to embrace the idea that life's complexity isn't something to solve—it's something to engage with. The more you lean into curiosity, the more you realize that every answer leads to new questions, every certainty holds room for expansion.

But curiosity isn't just a mindset—it's a practice. It's choosing to approach the moments that feel stuck or challenging with a spirit of exploration rather than resistance. What happens when you pause to wonder instead of rushing to react? What shifts when you ask *What can I learn here?* instead of *Why is this happening to me?* The act of wondering transforms the energy of tension into the energy of discovery, turning what feels impossible into something worth engaging with.

Curiosity also fosters connection. When you approach others with curiosity, you create space for understanding, for empathy, for connection that goes beyond surface interactions. What matters most to this person? What experiences have shaped their perspective? What would it mean to see the world through their eyes, even for a moment? Curiosity bridges the gap between you and others, reminding you that every person, like every moment, holds something new to discover.

To live with curiosity is to live expansively. It's to see the world not as a fixed set of rules or truths, but as a landscape of infinite possibilities, a canvas where each question adds depth and dimension. It's to remember that the gift of curiosity isn't just about finding answers—it's about finding yourself within the process of wondering, exploring, and becoming.

Chapter 10: The Strength of Vulnerability
Section A: Opening to Change

The Courage to Be Open

Vulnerability is often misunderstood. It's seen as a weakness, a crack in the armor, a risk to be avoided. But vulnerability isn't weakness—it's courage in its rawest form. To be vulnerable is to open yourself to life as it is, to show up fully and honestly, even when there are no guarantees. It's the willingness to be seen, not just in your strength, but in your uncertainty, your struggle, your becoming.

Opening to change requires vulnerability because change asks you to let go of control. It asks you to step into the unknown, to engage with the discomfort of not knowing what comes next. This openness isn't easy—it feels like standing in a storm without a map, without a shield. But vulnerability isn't about being defenseless—it's about being present. It's about choosing to stay open, even when fear and doubt whisper that it's safer to close off.

The courage to be open begins with accepting imperfection. Life doesn't demand that you have all the answers or that you navigate change flawlessly. It asks only that you show up, that you engage with what's happening, that you allow yourself to feel the full spectrum of your experience. Vulnerability doesn't mean exposing yourself to harm—it means being honest with yourself about what you're feeling, what you need, what matters most. It's about letting yourself be human.

Openness also means allowing others to see you as you are, not as you think you should be. This kind of vulnerability creates connection, not because it makes you invulnerable, but because it makes you real. When you allow yourself to be seen—your fears, your doubts, your hopes—you invite others to do the same. This mutual openness creates a rhythm of trust, a shared space where both people can grow, change, and support each other in the motion of life.

But vulnerability isn't just about connection—it's also about strength. It takes strength to admit when you're uncertain, when you're struggling, when you don't have it all figured out. It takes strength to open yourself to change, to trust that the process of becoming will carry you, even when you can't see the full path ahead. Vulnerability isn't a flaw—it's the foundation of resilience, the ability to adapt and grow through life's inevitable shifts.

To be open is to be brave. It's to say yes to life's motion, even when it feels unpredictable. It's to trust that the discomfort of vulnerability holds within it the potential for transformation. The courage to be open doesn't mean you won't feel fear—it means you'll choose to move forward anyway, knowing that the strength you need is already within you.

Trusting the Process

Vulnerability isn't just about showing up—it's about trusting the process of change, even when it feels uncertain or uncomfortable. To open yourself to life's motion is to accept that you won't always know the outcome, that you can't always predict where the path will lead. Trusting the process means believing that growth is happening, even when it's not immediately visible. It means staying open to the unfolding, allowing yourself to be shaped by what comes next.

Trusting the process begins with letting go of the need for control. It's natural to want to hold on tightly to what feels safe, to try to shape the future with precision and certainty. But control is often an illusion, and the tighter you grip, the more the flow of life resists. Vulnerability invites you to release that grip, to let go of the belief that you have to have all the answers, and to trust that the process itself will guide you toward what you need.

This trust doesn't mean passivity—it means engagement. Trusting the process asks you to show up fully, to participate in your own becoming, to take small, meaningful steps even when the bigger picture isn't clear. It's about focusing on what's within your reach, what you can do in this moment, while allowing the larger rhythm of life to carry you forward. Vulnerability doesn't erase uncertainty—it transforms it into possibility.

But trusting the process also means trusting yourself. It's about believing that you have the capacity to navigate whatever comes, that the strength and resilience you've built will support you in the face of change. It's about remembering that vulnerability isn't a sign of weakness—it's a sign of your willingness to engage with life fully, to move with its rhythm rather than resisting its flow. The process doesn't promise ease, but it promises growth—and that growth begins with trust.

Opening to change also asks you to trust others. Vulnerability isn't something you navigate alone—it's something you share.

When you trust the people around you with your fears, your hopes, your uncertainties, you create space for connection, for mutual support, for growth that is shared rather than solitary. Trusting others doesn't mean handing over your power—it means recognizing that connection is part of the process, that life's motion is something we navigate together.

To trust the process is to trust the motion of life itself. It's to believe that even when the path feels uncertain, even when the changes feel overwhelming, even when you don't yet see the full picture, the process is moving you toward something meaningful. Vulnerability is the strength to stay open in the face of that uncertainty, to let the process unfold, to trust that the motion is part of your becoming.

Section B: Resilience in Openness
The Power of Staying Open

Resilience is often imagined as toughness, as the ability to withstand pressure without breaking. But true resilience isn't about rigidity—it's about flexibility. It's about staying open to life's changes, even when they feel overwhelming. Resilience in openness means allowing yourself to bend, to adapt, to flow with the motion of life, trusting that openness doesn't weaken you—it strengthens you.

Staying open takes courage because it means allowing life to touch you deeply. It means engaging with the moments that challenge you, the emotions that unsettle you, the uncertainties that pull you into uncharted territory. To stay open is to choose presence over avoidance, curiosity over fear, engagement over retreat. It's to trust that you can remain open to the world without being consumed by it.

The power of staying open lies in its ability to transform. When you close yourself off, you cut yourself off—not just from pain, but from connection, from possibility, from growth. Openness creates space for these things to take root. It allows you to move through challenges rather than being held in place by them. It reminds you that the moments that feel the hardest are often the moments that carry the greatest potential for transformation.

Resilience in openness also means accepting imperfection. Staying open doesn't mean navigating life flawlessly—it means being willing to try, to stumble, to learn. It's about embracing the messy, imperfect process of becoming, trusting that the mistakes, the missteps, the moments of vulnerability are all part of the journey. Resilience isn't about avoiding the cracks—it's about letting the light in through them.

But staying open isn't just about enduring—it's about growing. Openness allows you to engage with the lessons that life is offering, to see the opportunities within the challenges, to discover strengths you didn't know you had. It's not about shielding yourself from pain—it's about finding meaning within it, about letting the discomfort of growth guide you toward something deeper, something truer, something more aligned.

To stay open is to trust yourself. It's to believe that you are strong enough to engage with life fully, even when it feels uncertain or uncomfortable. It's to remember that resilience isn't about being unbreakable—it's about being adaptable, about learning how to bend without losing your sense of who you are. Openness doesn't weaken you—it empowers you, allowing you to move with life's motion instead of resisting it.

Growing Through the Cracks

Resilience doesn't mean avoiding the cracks—it means growing through them. The moments when life feels fractured, when your plans unravel, when the path ahead seems unclear—these are not signs of weakness. They are openings, spaces where growth begins. To be resilient in openness is to embrace these cracks not as failures, but as opportunities to deepen, to expand, to become.

Growth through the cracks begins with acceptance. Life doesn't always go the way you expect, and the cracks remind you of that truth. But acceptance isn't the same as resignation. It doesn't mean giving up or settling for less—it means choosing to engage with life as it is, rather than clinging to what you think it should be. It means looking at the cracks and asking: *What is this moment asking of me? What new possibilities are hidden within this fracture?*

The cracks also reveal what's beneath the surface. They show you the parts of yourself that you've been hiding, the truths you've been avoiding, the strengths you didn't know you had. To grow through the cracks is to look into them with curiosity instead of fear, to explore what they're showing you about your values, your priorities, your capacity for resilience. The cracks aren't the end of the story—they're the place where the story shifts, where something new begins to take shape.

Resilience in openness also means staying connected. The cracks can feel isolating, like walls that separate you from the people and possibilities around you. But they can also be bridges— spaces where vulnerability creates connection, where honesty and authenticity invite others to join you in your journey. When you share your struggles, when you allow others to see your cracks, you create space for mutual growth, for relationships that are built not on perfection, but on trust.

To grow through the cracks is to trust the process of becoming. It's to believe that the fractures you're experiencing aren't breaking you—they're shaping you. They're creating space for light, for clarity, for something new to emerge. This growth isn't always visible in the moment, and it isn't always comfortable. But over time, the cracks begin to reveal their purpose, showing you the depth, the strength, the beauty that's been growing within you all along.

Resilience in openness is a choice—a choice to stay present with the cracks, to engage with the challenges, to trust that the discomfort of growth is worth it. It's a reminder that the cracks don't diminish you—they add texture, depth, and meaning to your life. To grow through the cracks is to embrace the truth that life's motion isn't here to break you—it's here to shape you. And in that shaping, you become.

Chapter 11: The Beauty of Becoming
Section A: Finding Depth in Motion
Layers of Growth

Becoming isn't about reaching a single, definitive version of yourself—it's about discovering the many layers that make up who you are. Each experience, each challenge, each moment of joy or tension adds depth to your life, shaping you in ways that aren't always immediately visible. The beauty of becoming lies in this layering, in the way life weaves together the moments of clarity and chaos, stillness and motion, creating a tapestry that is rich, dynamic, and alive.

Finding depth in motion means embracing the idea that growth doesn't happen in a straight line. It spirals, loops, and overlaps, bringing you back to familiar themes with new perspectives. The lessons you thought you'd learned resurface, not because you failed, but because you're ready to explore them on a deeper level. Each layer builds on the last, adding complexity, meaning, and understanding to the process of becoming.

Depth also comes from engagement. Life doesn't ask you to have everything figured out—it asks you to show up, to participate, to move with its rhythm even when the steps feel uncertain. The layers of growth aren't something you achieve by standing still —they're something you create by being present with life as it unfolds, by engaging with its challenges and opportunities, by allowing yourself to be shaped by its motion.

But finding depth in motion isn't just about looking forward—it's also about looking back. The layers of your life don't exist in isolation—they're connected, woven together into a larger story. To find depth is to revisit the moments that have shaped you, to honor the lessons they've taught, and to carry their wisdom into the present. It's about seeing how the layers of your past inform the choices you make now, how they add dimension to the person you are becoming.

The depth of becoming also asks for presence. Growth isn't something that happens all at once—it happens in the small moments, the quiet shifts, the everyday choices that add up over time. To find depth in motion is to slow down enough to notice these moments, to appreciate the subtle ways they shape you, to recognize that the beauty of becoming isn't in the destination but in the process itself.

To live with depth is to embrace life's complexity, to see its layers not as something to fix or simplify, but as something to explore. It's to trust that the motion you're in—the spirals, the loops, the returns—isn't taking you away from yourself but bringing you closer. The beauty of becoming isn't in arriving—it's in the unfolding, the layering, the depth that grows with each step, each moment, each choice.

Embracing the Layers

To truly embrace the beauty of becoming, you must learn to value the layers of your life—not just the ones that feel smooth and certain, but the ones that carry tension, complexity, and questions. Each layer represents a piece of your journey, a moment of discovery, a step along the path of growth. The layers don't always align perfectly, and they don't always make sense in the moment. But together, they form the texture of a life that is dynamic, authentic, and deeply human.

Embracing the layers begins with acceptance. Growth doesn't happen in neat stages—it's messy, nonlinear, and often surprising. The layers of your life don't always unfold in the order you expect, and they rarely bring immediate clarity. But this unpredictability is part of what makes becoming so rich. Each layer holds something valuable, even when it feels incomplete or unresolved. To embrace the layers is to trust that the meaning will emerge in time, that the process itself is where the depth lies.

Depth also comes from integration. The layers of your life aren't separate—they're interconnected, influencing and shaping each other in ways you might not always see. The choices you made years ago ripple into the decisions you face today. The lessons you've learned in one part of your life inform the way you approach challenges in another. To integrate the layers is to see them not as isolated pieces, but as part of a larger whole, a continuous unfolding of who you are.

But embracing the layers isn't just about looking back—it's also about looking forward. The beauty of becoming lies in its openness, its invitation to keep adding layers, to keep exploring, to keep growing. What new experiences might shape you next? What perspectives are waiting to be uncovered? What layers will you create as you continue to move, to learn, to become? The process of layering is never finished—it's a lifelong journey, a rhythm of adding depth and meaning to your life with each passing moment.

This embrace also requires compassion. Not every layer will feel beautiful at first. Some will feel heavy, jagged, difficult to hold. But these layers are no less important. They add dimension, texture, resilience. They remind you that becoming isn't about perfection —it's about wholeness. To embrace the layers is to see each one as essential, as part of the larger story of who you are and who you are becoming.

To live with depth is to honor the layers of your life, to recognize that the spirals, the loops, the returns are not detours—they're the path itself. It's to see the beauty not just in the moments of clarity, but in the moments of tension, transformation, and growth. The layers don't take you away from yourself—they bring you closer, revealing the richness, the complexity, the beauty of your becoming.

Section B: A Life in Progress
Becoming Without End

To be alive is to be in progress. The work of becoming doesn't have a finish line, a final moment where you arrive fully formed and complete. Instead, it is an ongoing process, a rhythm of growth and change that continues throughout your life. This truth is both freeing and humbling: freeing because it reminds you that you don't have to have everything figured out, and humbling because it shows you that there will always be more to learn, more to explore, more to become.

A life in progress isn't about constant striving—it's about constant engagement. It's about showing up for the motion of life, not as a means to an end but as an experience in itself. The process of becoming isn't something you endure to get somewhere—it's something you participate in fully, moment by moment. It's the decisions you make, the connections you nurture, the way you respond to life's surprises and challenges. Becoming isn't about what you achieve—it's about how you live.

But progress doesn't always feel linear. It loops and spirals, moving forward and doubling back, revealing new layers of understanding even as it revisits old questions. To live a life in progress is to embrace this rhythm, to see the returns not as failures but as opportunities to deepen your growth. The lessons you thought you'd learned reappear, not because you haven't grown but because you're ready to engage with them in new ways. The questions you thought you'd answered resurface, inviting you to explore them from a different angle, with a broader perspective.

Living in progress also means letting go of the need for permanence. Progress isn't about reaching a point where everything stays the same—it's about learning to adapt, to move with life's changes, to trust the motion even when it feels uncertain. It's about recognizing that stability and dissonance, clarity and chaos, are not endpoints but forces that shape the rhythm of your becoming. The beauty of progress lies in its motion, in its ability to keep you alive to the possibilities of the moment.

But a life in progress isn't just about growth—it's about presence. It's about being fully engaged with where you are, even as you remain open to where you're going. It's about finding joy in the journey, meaning in the motion, depth in the process of becoming. Progress doesn't ask you to be perfect—it asks you to be present, to bring your full self to the path you're walking, to trust that the steps you're taking are enough.

To be in progress is to embrace the truth that becoming is never finished, and that's not a flaw—it's a gift. It's the reminder that life is dynamic, that growth is endless, that you are always in the process of unfolding, discovering, creating. A life in progress isn't about arriving—it's about becoming, again and again, with each moment, each choice, each step.

Finding Meaning in the Motion

Becoming isn't about reaching a final destination—it's about finding meaning within the motion. Life's journey is not a straight path, nor is it a race to be won. It is a rhythm, a dance, a dynamic unfolding where meaning isn't something you discover at the end but something you create along the way. To live a life in progress is to embrace this truth, to see the motion itself as the source of life's richness and depth.

Finding meaning in motion begins with presence. It's about engaging with the moments you're in, even when they feel small, ordinary, or incomplete. The act of becoming happens not in grand gestures but in the quiet decisions, the everyday choices, the way you show up for yourself and others. These moments, though fleeting, are where meaning is created. They remind you that progress isn't measured by the distance you've traveled but by the fullness with which you've lived each step.

This meaning also comes from the connections you make. Life in motion isn't something you navigate alone—it's something you share with the people around you. The relationships you build, the ways you support and are supported, the experiences you create together—all of these add texture to your becoming. They remind you that the motion isn't just about you—it's about how you engage with the larger web of connection, how you contribute to the growth of others as you grow yourself.

But finding meaning in the motion also requires reflection. Progress doesn't always feel forward, and the spirals, loops, and returns can make it easy to lose sight of how far you've come. Reflection allows you to pause, to look back at the path you've walked, and to recognize the layers of growth and understanding that have accumulated over time. It reminds you that even when the motion feels chaotic, it has been shaping you, guiding you, deepening your sense of who you are.

Meaning in motion also comes from embracing uncertainty.

Life's rhythm is unpredictable, and the motion often takes you in directions you didn't expect. But within this uncertainty lies possibility. When you stop trying to control every step and start trusting the flow, you create space for the unexpected, for opportunities and insights you couldn't have planned for. The motion isn't something to resist—it's something to engage with, to let it carry you toward the unknown with curiosity and courage.

To live a life in progress is to let go of the need for a fixed endpoint and to find meaning in the motion itself. It's to see the beauty in the unfolding, the growth in the spirals, the depth in the layers that continue to accumulate. It's to trust that the process of becoming is enough, that the motion is part of what makes life alive, vibrant, and meaningful. A life in progress isn't about arriving—it's about becoming, and in that becoming, you find not just who you are but who you are always in the process of becoming.

Chapter 12: The Infinite Dance
Section A: Motion as Harmony

The Rhythm of Life

Harmony isn't found in stillness—it's found in motion. Life doesn't pause to offer you a perfect moment of clarity or balance. It moves, continuously, weaving together the opposites, the tensions, the shifts that create its rhythm. To find harmony is not to escape the motion but to live within it, to embrace the constant flow as the very thing that gives life its meaning, its beauty, its depth.

The rhythm of life is dynamic, never fixed. It ebbs and flows, rises and falls, creating patterns that are both familiar and unpredictable. Some moments surge forward with clarity and energy, while others retreat into stillness and reflection. This rhythm isn't random—it's responsive, shaped by the interplay of your actions, your choices, your emotions. To live in harmony is to move with this rhythm, to trust its patterns, to let its motion guide you.

But harmony in motion isn't about perfection. It's not about always being in sync or always knowing the next step. It's about presence, about showing up for the rhythm as it is, not as you wish it would be. Some moments will feel smooth and effortless, while others will feel uneven, even chaotic. Harmony doesn't erase the tension—it integrates it, allowing the opposites, the contradictions, the dissonance to become part of the rhythm, part of the dance.

The rhythm of life also asks for adaptability. To live in harmony, you must be willing to adjust, to recalibrate, to shift your tempo as the rhythm changes. This isn't about abandoning your direction—it's about staying flexible, staying open, staying engaged with the motion. Harmony isn't a static state—it's a dynamic process, one that requires you to move with life rather than resisting it.

Living in harmony also means letting go of the idea that you can control the rhythm. The motion of life isn't something you dictate—it's something you collaborate with. It's a partnership between your intentions and life's unpredictability, between your desires and the opportunities that unfold. Harmony isn't about forcing the rhythm to fit your expectations—it's about finding your place within it, learning to flow with its motion, trusting that it will carry you forward.

The rhythm of life is the infinite dance of becoming, a dance that holds both joy and sorrow, light and shadow, clarity and dissonance. To find harmony is not to master the rhythm—it's to move with it, to let it guide you, to let it shape you. The motion isn't something to overcome—it's the very thing that makes the dance possible.

Flowing with Life

To flow with life is to step into the infinite dance, to engage with the rhythm not as something to master but as something to live within. The motion of life is constant—it doesn't wait for you to feel ready or for everything to align perfectly. It carries you, sometimes gently, sometimes forcefully, but always forward. Harmony isn't about stopping the motion—it's about flowing with it, trusting that the rhythm will support you as you move.

Flowing with life begins with letting go of resistance. It's natural to want to hold on to what feels familiar, to cling to stability, to try to control the direction of the current. But resistance only creates friction, making the motion feel harder, heavier, more chaotic. To flow is to release the need for control, to trust that life's rhythm will guide you, even when the path isn't clear. It's about leaning into the motion rather than pushing against it.

But flowing doesn't mean being passive—it means being present. To flow with life is to engage fully with its motion, to participate in the rhythm rather than letting it carry you unconsciously. It's about noticing the patterns, the cycles, the shifts, and choosing how to move within them. Where is the current asking you to go? What adjustments can you make to align with its flow? What opportunities are hidden within the motion, waiting for you to reach for them? Flowing isn't about letting life happen to you—it's about creating with it.

Flowing with life also means embracing its unpredictability. The rhythm isn't always smooth, and the current doesn't always follow a straight line. There will be moments of turbulence, times when the motion feels overwhelming or disorienting. These moments aren't interruptions—they're part of the rhythm, part of the dance. To flow is to stay present even in the uncertainty, to trust that the motion will carry you, to believe that each turn, each shift, each rise and fall is part of a larger pattern.

Harmony in motion also asks for trust—not just in life, but

in yourself. It's about believing that you have the capacity to navigate the rhythm, that you can move with the changes, that you can find your balance even when the motion feels intense. Flowing with life isn't about avoiding the tension—it's about letting it guide you, letting it deepen your understanding of the rhythm, letting it become part of the dance.

To flow with life is to embrace the infinite dance of becoming. It's to see the motion not as something to fear but as something to celebrate, to trust that each step, each choice, each moment of movement brings you closer to the harmony you're creating. The rhythm isn't taking you away from yourself—it's bringing you deeper into who you are. And in that motion, in that dance, you find not just harmony—you find life itself.

Section B: Becoming as Being
The Ongoing Journey

Becoming isn't something you finish—it's something you are. To be alive is to be in motion, constantly growing, learning, and evolving. Becoming isn't a task to complete or a destination to reach—it's the essence of being itself. It's the rhythm of your existence, the infinite unfolding of who you are and who you are becoming, moment by moment, choice by choice.

The ongoing journey of becoming begins with acceptance. Life isn't static, and neither are you. The person you were yesterday is not the person you are today, and the person you are today will not be the person you are tomorrow. This isn't a flaw—it's a gift. To be in motion is to be alive, to have the opportunity to keep exploring, discovering, and shaping yourself in ways that reflect your deepest truths. Becoming isn't about achieving a fixed identity—it's about engaging with the process of being fully and authentically.

This journey also requires presence. Becoming doesn't happen in the abstract—it happens in the everyday moments, the small choices, the quiet shifts that shape your life over time. It's easy to focus on the big milestones, the visible markers of progress, and overlook the subtle ways you're growing with each passing moment. But the beauty of becoming lies in the present, in the way you show up for yourself and the world right now. It's about being here, fully engaged with the motion of life as it unfolds.

The ongoing nature of becoming also invites you to embrace imperfection. To be in motion is to be unfinished, to carry within you the tension of what you've been and what you're becoming. This tension isn't something to resolve—it's something to live within, to let it guide you toward the deeper alignment that emerges when you stay open to growth. Imperfection isn't a limitation—it's the space where creativity, discovery, and authenticity thrive.

But becoming isn't just about the self—it's about connection. Your journey is intertwined with the journeys of others, and the rhythm of your becoming often echoes within the relationships and communities that shape your life. What does your motion inspire in others? How does their motion influence you? Becoming isn't a solitary act—it's a shared dance, one that invites you to engage with the collective rhythm of growth, understanding, and connection.

To live as someone who is becoming is to embrace the infinite nature of the journey. It's to let go of the need for finality, for certainty, for resolution, and to trust that the motion itself is enough. Becoming isn't about arriving—it's about being, fully and completely, within the rhythm of your life. And in that being, you discover not just who you are, but the endless possibilities of who you are becoming.

Living the Dance

To live the dance of becoming is to step fully into the flow of life, embracing its motion as a constant, dynamic rhythm. Becoming isn't something separate from being—it's the act of living itself, the ongoing interplay between who you are and who you are becoming. This dance isn't about perfection or completion—it's about participation, about engaging with the motion of life as it unfolds, moment by moment.

Living the dance begins with presence. The motion of becoming doesn't happen in the abstract—it happens in the choices you make, the connections you nurture, the way you show up for yourself and others. It's in the moments of tension, where clarity feels distant but growth feels possible. It's in the moments of joy, where alignment feels effortless and motion feels natural. To live the dance is to embrace each moment as part of the rhythm, trusting that even the smallest steps are part of a larger motion.

But living the dance also requires humility. Becoming isn't about having all the answers or knowing exactly where the rhythm will take you. It's about staying open, staying curious, staying willing to move even when the path ahead feels uncertain. The dance isn't linear, and it isn't predictable. It loops, spirals, and shifts, inviting you to adapt, to recalibrate, to grow. To live the dance is to trust that the motion itself is meaningful, even when you can't see the full pattern.

This trust also extends to yourself. To live the dance is to believe in your capacity to move with life's rhythm, even when it feels challenging or unfamiliar. It's to recognize that resilience doesn't come from resisting the motion but from flowing with it, from allowing yourself to be carried by the rhythm rather than trying to control it. The dance isn't something you master—it's something you live, something you create with each step, each choice, each moment of engagement.

Living the dance also means embracing connection. The rhythm of your life doesn't exist in isolation—it's part of a larger symphony, a collective motion that includes the people, the communities, the world around you. To live the dance is to engage with this collective rhythm, to see how your motion influences and is influenced by others. It's about recognizing that the dance of becoming isn't just personal—it's shared, a dynamic interplay that creates harmony within the motion of life itself.

The dance of becoming isn't about finding a fixed state of being—it's about celebrating the motion. It's about seeing the cracks, the tension, the uncertainty not as obstacles but as the spaces where growth happens, where meaning is created, where life becomes alive. The dance doesn't end—it continues, unfolding in layers, deepening with each step, revealing the endless possibilities of who you are and who you are becoming.

To live the dance is to embrace the infinite nature of being. It's to let go of the need to arrive and to trust that the motion itself is the destination. It's to see the beauty not just in the moments of clarity but in the moments of chaos, not just in the moments of joy but in the moments of tension. The dance isn't about where you're going—it's about how you move, how you create, how you become. And in that becoming, you discover that the motion isn't just something you live within—it's something you are.

Epilogue:
The Dance Goes On

Life doesn't stop moving. The rhythm of becoming continues, a constant interplay of stability and dissonance, clarity and chaos, motion and stillness. To live is to engage with this rhythm, to embrace its complexity, to trust that the dance of life is not something to master but something to live fully. Becoming is not an endpoint—it is a way of being.

This triadic journey—*Everything's OK, Not OK?,* and *Becoming OK* —has been a reflection of life's rhythm. It began with stability, with the recognition that alignment and clarity are possible, even amidst complexity. It moved into dissonance, exploring the cracks, the tension, the moments when alignment falters and chaos takes hold. And now it embraces motion, celebrating the dynamic process of becoming, the ongoing creation of harmony within life's infinite flux.

The dance of becoming isn't always graceful. There will be stumbles, moments when the rhythm feels out of reach, when the tension feels overwhelming. But these moments are not failures— they are part of the dance. They remind you that life's beauty lies not in perfection but in participation. The motion itself is what makes the dance meaningful, what gives it depth, what creates the harmony that holds both joy and sorrow, growth and struggle.

To live the dance is to honor its rhythm. It's to see the stability not as a place to stay but as a place to move from, the dissonance not as a problem to fix but as a force to create with, the motion not as a challenge to overcome but as a rhythm to flow within. The dance isn't something that happens to you—it's something you are. Each step, each choice, each moment of engagement is part of the rhythm, part of the unfolding, part of the infinite dance of becoming.

The journey doesn't end here. It continues, spiraling forward, inviting you to keep moving, to keep exploring, to keep creating the life that feels most true to who you are. Becoming isn't about arriving—it's about living, fully and authentically, within the motion of life. The dance goes on, and so do you.

May you trust the rhythm, honor the tension, and find harmony in the motion. May you celebrate the dance of becoming, knowing that within its rhythm lies the beauty, the depth, and the infinite possibility of life itself. And may you remember, always, that the dance isn't something you do—it's something you are.

B.T.C.

24-12-24

Aimee,

Dance in Love & Light

Brooke.

Printed in Great Britain
by Amazon